Real Life: Daredevils

Written by Nick Hunter

T0351242

Contents

Don't Try This at Home!

Get ready to meet the daredevils. These amazing people push themselves and their bodies to the limit. They amaze their fans with daring **stunts** that would be too terrifying and dangerous for most of us. Daredevils are always looking for new thrills to test their skill and courage.

The stunts in this book could seriously damage your health. Leave them to the experts!

For a daredevil, taking risks is part of the job.

Risky Business

The first daredevils performed with circuses or created stunts for fun. As new machines helped people move faster or fly higher, daredevils went faster and higher too. Fearless pilots performed astonishing tricks in the first aeroplanes. Later, daredevils used cars and motorcycles for jumping instead of driving.

Daredevil Yves Rossy built his own jet suit. Its four engines helped him fly 24 miles (around 38 kilometers) across the English Channel.

Sometimes daredevils go too far by breaking laws that are made to keep people safe. When things go wrong, daredevils risk serious injury and even death.

Harry Houdini

FACT FILE

- **Real name:** Ehrich Weiss
- **Date of birth:** 24th March 1874
- **Nationality:** Hungarian / American
- **Famous for:** amazing escapes from chains, locked boxes and worse
- **Riskiest stunt:** escaping from his chains in a locked box, underwater in New York's East River
- **Hobby:** swimming, which helped Harry build up his strength
- **Before he was famous:** Harry performed as a trapeze artist when he was nine years old

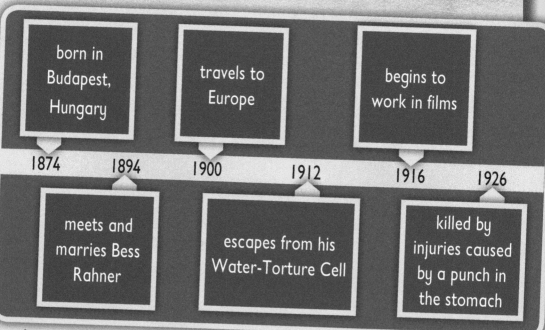

born in Budapest, Hungary

travels to Europe

begins to work in films

1874 1894 1900 1912 1916 1926

meets and marries Bess Rahner

escapes from his Water-Torture Cell

killed by injuries caused by a punch in the stomach

The World's Greatest

At the height of his fame, everyone knew Harry Houdini's name. He was the world's greatest escape artist. His **death-defying** stunts made newspaper headlines around the world.

From Hungary to Houdini

Harry's Jewish family moved from Budapest, Hungary, to the USA shortly after his birth. When he was 13 years old, Harry found a job cutting cloth for ties but he dreamed of being a magician. In 1891, he and a friend began to perform magic tricks as the Houdini Brothers. Later, his younger brother Theo joined them.

Harry took the stage name "Houdini" from one of his heroes. Jean-Eugène Robert-Houdin was a great French magician.

Harry started to perform magic after seeing a magician in a travelling circus.

5

Extreme Escapes

The Houdini Brothers invented some amazing tricks. The most exciting part of their **act** was magically swapping places in a locked trunk. But it was hard work attracting crowds, even to watch Harry's escapes from handcuffs.

In 1894, Harry met and married Bess Rahner. Bess also became Harry's assistant. Together they **toured** the USA, along with circus stars such as Blue Eagle who smashed boards over his head.

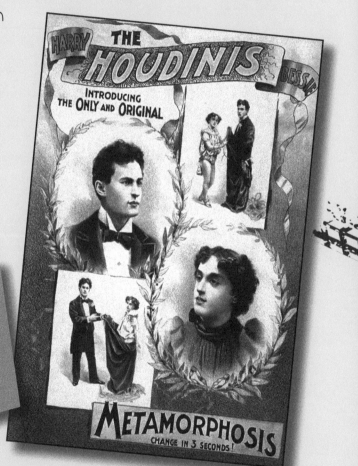

Bess' small size was perfect for a magician's assistant. It was easy for her to get in and out of boxes.

Harry's Big Prison Break

Harry plotted ways to get his escape act noticed. He invited some newspaper reporters to watch him escape from a Chicago prison. The next morning, Harry's photo was in the papers. His escape act was quickly hired for a tour of theatres all over the world. Harry and Bess' days as struggling magicians were over.

Politiepost. Halvemaansteeg Amsterdam Holland Jan 12 1905
HARRY HOUDINI was Stripped Stark Naked, Searched and heavily handcuffed and Legironed. He was then locked up in a Cell and in less than 5 minutes managed to free himself from the Cell and Handcuffs in an unexplainable manner.
Signed. Hoof Comm. Ed W van Roalte.
Chief of Police
D. J G. Vreede. Comm. Politie. C. Battel. Jvd Pals. A Krumner's.
H. J. Diederiks

HOUDINI in the Amsterdam (Holland) Prison Jan. 1902
BROKE OUT OF THE IRONS & CELL IN 15 MINUTES.

Harry took his shirt and trousers off to show people that he wasn't hiding any tools. But he often hid keys in his hair!

On one circus tour, Harry's handcuff escapes were much less popular than his "wild man" performance, where he ate raw meat and growled at the audience!

7

The Handcuff King

In 1900, Harry and Bess set out for London. Harry's fame soon spread and excited crowds filled theatres across Europe. Audience members brought their own handcuffs and chains to challenge the great **escapologist**. Harry would take his time, building the **suspense** but he always escaped in the end.

Harry needed to be very, very strong to escape from chains and **straitjackets**. Harry trained all his life and his muscles were said to be as hard as iron.

In 1905, Harry returned to the USA. While he had been away, new escapologists had started to copy his act. He needed something new.

Handcuffs and ball and chains were a key part of many of Harry's escape acts.

Life on the Line

Harry developed a new act in which he escaped from a large milk can full of water. Excitement grew as crowds wondered whether he would survive.

Harry's milk can escape was easier than it looked:
1. The can contained enough air for Harry to breathe for a short time
2. The top of the can seemed secure but was only loosely fixed
3. Harry lifted off the top to make his escape.

Harry's stunts got more spectacular. In 1912, Harry was handcuffed inside a sealed box and lowered into New York's East River. Less than a minute later, he burst out of the water to cheers from the 100,000 people watching from the shore.

9

Hollywood Harry

Silent films began to replace the live theatres where Harry had found fame. He decided to become a film star. Unfortunately, Harry was not a great actor, even in silent films. His film career was a short one!

Harry's films involved many daring stunts.

No Escape

Harry would let people punch him in the stomach to prove how strong he was. In October 1926, he was punched while resting backstage. Harry was not ready, and the blow burst his appendix. He died soon afterwards.

Harry Houdini's name is still used to describe anyone who escapes from an impossible situation. His daring inspired other daredevils and magicians.

Bessie Coleman

FACT FILE

- **Real name:** Elizabeth Coleman
- **Date of birth:** 26th January 1892
- **Nationality:** American
- **Famous for:** being the first black female stunt pilot
- **Riskiest stunt: loop-the-loop** in a "Jenny" **biplane**
- **Hobby:** parachuting, which she sometimes included in her stunt displays
- **Before she was famous:** Bessie trained to work in a beauty salon!

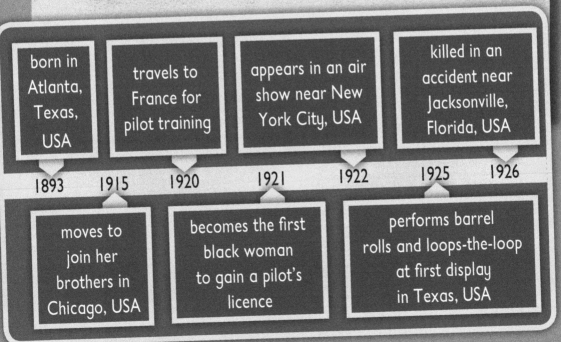

born in Atlanta, Texas, USA

travels to France for pilot training

appears in an air show near New York City, USA

killed in an accident near Jacksonville, Florida, USA

1893   1915   1920   1921   1922   1925   1926

moves to join her brothers in Chicago, USA

becomes the first black woman to gain a pilot's licence

performs barrel rolls and loops-the-loop at first display in Texas, USA

Fighting for Survival

Bessie Coleman was one of the world's first stunt pilots. Her fight to become a pilot was just as amazing as her tricks in the sky.

A Tough Start

Bessie was born in Atlanta, Texas. In the southern USA at this time, people with black skin were not treated the same as people with white skin.

Bessie studied hard at school but family life made it difficult for her to go to school. She had to help her mother care for her three younger sisters, as well as work in the cotton fields.

When Bessie was ten years old, Wilbur and Orville Wright flew the world's first proper aeroplane. Bessie saw early aircraft in books and films and she longed to fly planes too.

Chasing the Dream

Bessie was determined to become a pilot but there were two problems: there were very few women pilots, and no black women pilots at all!

Bessie was rejected by all the flying schools in the country but she would not take "no" for an answer. She saved her money and sailed to France to train as a pilot. In 1921, Bessie became the first black woman to get a pilot's licence.

As well as gaining her pilot's licence, Bessie learned to do stunts in a Nieuport biplane like this one.

Barnstorming

When Bessie returned from France, people could not wait to see the new flying acrobat. Thousands of people came to see her first appearance at an air show near New York City in 1922.

Bessie began flying in "barnstorming" air shows. Barnstormers were people who performed daring stunts in the air. As Bessie rolled her plane over and looped-the-loop, she proved that she was as good as any male pilot in the air.

Barnstorming shows also featured brave **wing walkers.**

In 1923, Bessie was badly injured in a crash. She had to have a year away from flying, just as her career was really taking off.

Famous Flyer

Bessie's thrilling performances made her a celebrity. She never forgot the problems she had overcome to become famous. Wherever she performed, she always tried to make sure that black and white spectators were treated the same and could sit together.

Bessie also learned to do parachute jumps and added these to her displays.

Bessie receiving flowers after another exciting air show.

Flying into Danger

Flying planes in the 1920s was very dangerous. There were few safety rules and crashes were common. The "Jenny" aircraft used by barnstormers like Bessie had to fly especially low so spectators could see the stunts properly.

Tragic Accident

On 30th April 1926, Bessie was preparing for her next show. She was flying with her engineer when he lost control of the plane. Bessie was not wearing a seatbelt. She was thrown out of the plane and she died in the accident. Thousands of people came to the funeral of this **pioneering** pilot.

Bessie with one of her planes.

In 2000, Bessie's life was celebrated when her image appeared on a US stamp.

A True Daredevil

Bessie had to be brave and determined to achieve her dream of flying planes. Her career ended in tragedy, but Bessie had already proved herself to be one of the bravest daredevils of all.

Bessie's stunts inspired many who saw her. Black **aviators** founded the Bessie Coleman Aero Club and took part in air shows.

Some daredevils still perform in planes like the ones made famous by Bessie.

Evel Knievel

FACT FILE

- **Real name:** Robert Knievel
- **Date of birth:** 17th October 1938
- **Nationality:** American
- **Famous for:** being a motorcycle stunt rider
- **Riskiest stunt:** attempting to jump the Snake River Canyon, Idaho, USA
- **Hobby:** sports such as athletics, ski jumping, and ice hockey
- **Before he was famous:** Evel worked in copper and diamond mines

born in Butte, Montana, USA

jumps the fountains outside Caesar's Palace, Las Vegas, USA

attempts to jump Snake River Canyon in rocket-powered Sky Cycle

dies in Clearwater, Florida, USA

1938   1965   1967   1973   1974   1977   2007

first jump to promote motorcycle store in Butte, USA

jumps over 50 cars in the Los Angeles Coliseum

stars in Hollywood film *Viva Knievel!*

Motorcycle Master

Evel Knievel was one of the most popular daredevils of all time. People were thrilled by his daring motorbike jumps over everything from buses to sharks.

Becoming Evel

Robert Knievel was born in Montana, USA. He was nicknamed "Evil" Knievel by local police because he often got into trouble but he changed the spelling to "Evel". In the 1950s, Evel joined the army and trained to be a parachutist.

Evel knew what he wanted to do after seeing stunt-car driver Joie Chitwood's *Thrill Show* in the 1950s. The live shows featured high-speed car jumps and stunts.

Joie Chitwood began his daredevil career as a racing driver.

Crowds and Crashes

By 1965, Evel owned a motorcycle shop. He invited customers to watch him jump his motorcycle over parked cars and a box of rattlesnakes. Despite landing on the rattlesnakes, Evel liked the thrill and the cheers of the crowd. He wanted to try bigger and riskier jumps.

Evel formed the Evel Knievel Motorcycle Daredevils. He was a natural **showman** and soon started to perform on his own. His fame spread worldwide after he jumped the fountains at Caesar's Palace Casino in Las Vegas, even though the jump ended in a horrific crash.

Evel's jump and crash at Caesar's Palace was filmed and shown around the world.

Rocket Man

In 1974, Evel prepared to jump the Snake River Canyon, on a steam-powered rocket called the Sky Cycle. The rocket soared out over the canyon, but its parachute opened too soon. Evel and the rocket floated down to land safely at the bottom of the canyon.

Evel's Sky Cycle was designed to soar over the canyon at 350 miles per hour (560 kilometres per hour).

During his life, Evel had at least 15 major operations to fix broken bones. He even broke some of the metal plates and pins that held his damaged bones together!

21

Death-defying Jumps

In 1975, Evel attempted his first jump outside the USA. In front of a packed crowd in London's Wembley Stadium, he tried to jump over a world-record 13 buses!

The crowd went quiet as his bike flew across the row of buses. But as he landed, Evel lost control of his bike and crashed. In agony from his injuries, Evel said that Wembley would be his last jump. However, a few months later he was back on his bike!

When he crashed in London, Evel was badly injured when his motorcycle landed on top of him.

Jumping Sharks

Evel looked for even more dangerous stunts after his lucky escape in London. In 1976, Evel planned to jump over a tank full of sharks. During a practice jump he made it over the tank but, once again, injured himself in a crash landing.

Evel cancelled his shark jump after the practice jump crash.

By the late 1970s, Evel's star-studded suit was recognised around the world. His death-defying jumps made him a hero to millions of people.

Evel's jumps were exciting because there was a good chance they might go wrong — and they often did.

Motorcycle Madness

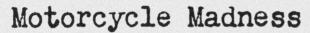

Evel broke almost every bone in his body as he tried to make more and more spectacular jumps. But, unlike many daredevils, he lived long enough to tell the tale. Evel retired in 1980. He died in 2007, aged 69.

Evel inspired many daredevils who followed in his tracks. His son Robbie Knievel also does daring motorcycle jumps. Robbie would like to beat Evel's record by jumping 16 buses.

In 1999, Robbie Knievel jumped almost 70 metres across part of the Grand Canyon, USA.

Alain Robert

FACT FILE

- **Real name:** Alain Robert
- **Date of birth:** 7th August 1962
- **Nationality:** French
- **Famous for:** climbing **skyscrapers** without safety gear
- **Riskiest stunt:** climbing the world's tallest building
- **Hobby:** climbing – Alain's hobby is also his job!
- **Before he was famous:** Alain was scared of heights as a child. Climbing helped him to beat this fear.

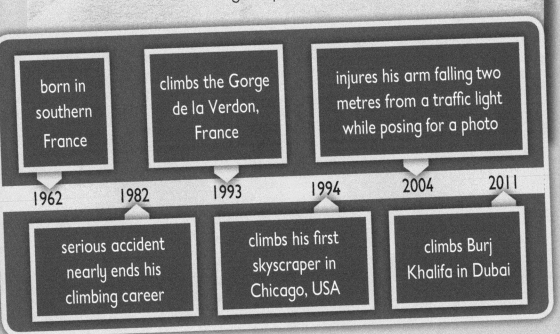

| 1962 | 1982 | 1993 | 1994 | 2004 | 2011 |

born in southern France

climbs the Gorge de la Verdon, France

injures his arm falling two metres from a traffic light while posing for a photo

serious accident nearly ends his climbing career

climbs his first skyscraper in Chicago, USA

climbs Burj Khalifa in Dubai

The Real Spiderman

Everyone knows Spiderman isn't real. Only a superhero could climb up the **sheer** sides of city skyscrapers using nothing but his bare hands. He may not usually dress like Spiderman, but there is a man who has proved it is possible to climb the world's tallest buildings. His name is Alain Robert.

Head for Heights

Alain was born in the south of France. He was fascinated by climbing and began to climb on the rocks around his hometown. At the age of 11, he forgot his door key and climbed 15 metres to his bedroom on the seventh floor.

Alain once dressed as Spiderman to climb a skyscraper in Shanghai, China.

No Safety Net

Alain is a rock climber with a twist. Other climbers use ropes and harnesses to keep them safe, but Alain climbs with his bare hands and no support. Without a rope, one false move could be **fatal**.

Alain's heroes were the climbers who tackled the most difficult mountains and rock faces in the nearby **Alps**. When Alain tried these climbs himself, he was disappointed to find they were a bit too easy!

Climbing without any ropes or safety gear is called "free soloing".

Brush with Death

Although Alain normally climbs using his bare hands, his most serious accident happened in 1982, when a rope he was using gave way. He fell 15 metres and landed on his head. It was a year before he could climb again.

Most climbers use ropes to help them climb sheer rock faces.

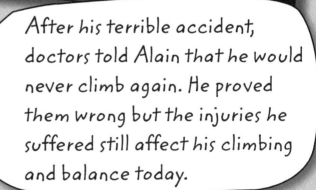

After his terrible accident, doctors told Alain that he would never climb again. He proved them wrong but the injuries he suffered still affect his climbing and balance today.

Scaling Skyscrapers

In 1994, Alain was looking for new climbing challenges. A film-maker wanted to film him climbing a skyscraper in Chicago, USA. From the ground, it seemed impossible. A concrete and glass building has almost nothing for a climber to grip on to. But the climb was a success and Alain went looking for even taller buildings.

Alain went on to climb nearly 100 skyscrapers around the world. His amazing climbs take between two and four hours. He faces many dangers, including the weather. Rain or mist can make the glass sides of a skyscraper very slippery.

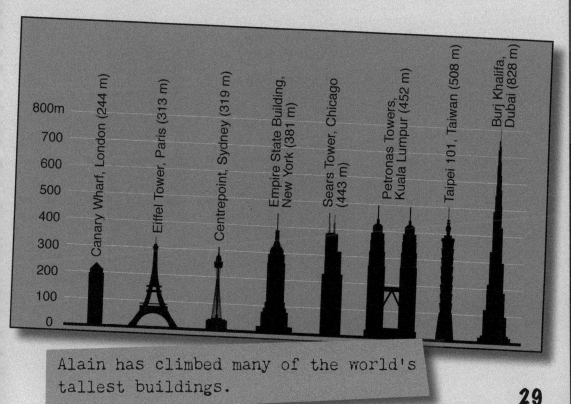

Alain has climbed many of the world's tallest buildings.

Reaching New Heights

Alain's daring climbs have brought him worldwide fame. Building owners and businesses often ask him to climb their buildings and huge crowds gather to watch the amazing human spider.

Alain's stunts are not popular with everyone. He has been arrested many times for climbing buildings without permission, and for breaking safety rules.

rubber-soled shoes

Alain normally climbs with nothing more than rubber-soled shoes and some chalk dust to help him grip.

a bag for chalk dust

Top of the World

In March 2011, Alain made his riskiest climb yet. He climbed the world's tallest building in Dubai. There may not be any new mountains to climb but there will always be new buildings to test this daredevil!

Alain reached the spire of the 828 metre Burj Khalifa after six hours of climbing.

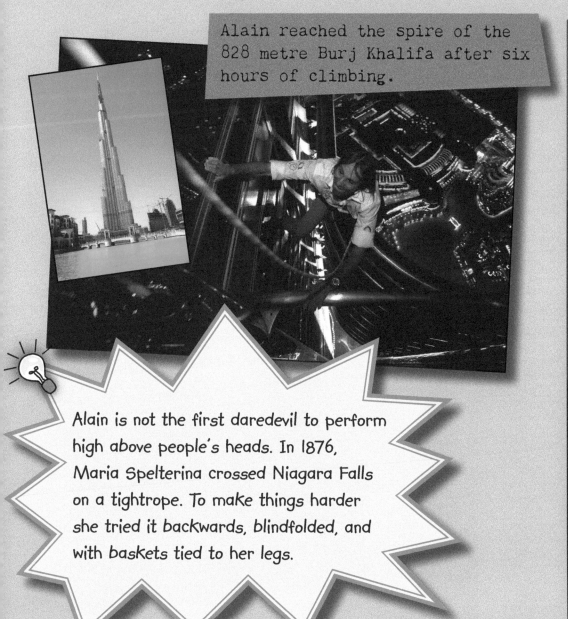

Alain is not the first daredevil to perform high above people's heads. In 1876, Maria Spelterina crossed Niagara Falls on a tightrope. To make things harder she tried it backwards, blindfolded, and with baskets tied to her legs.

Glossary

act performance, such as a show put on by a magician

Alps mountain range in Europe

aviators pilots

biplane plane with two pairs of wings

death-defying way to describe actions in which the performer risks death

escapologist performer who escapes from very difficult situations

fatal leading to death

loop-the-loop when an aeroplane is flown in a circle in the air

pioneering being the first person to do something

sheer nearly vertical

showman person who likes to entertain people, such as a circus performer

skyscraper very tall building with many different floors

straitjackets strong items of clothing that stop you from moving your arms

stunts tricks or daring performances

suspense excitedly waiting for something that is about to happen

toured performed in different places

wing walkers people who perform stunts on the wings of flying aeroplanes

Index